Original title:

Sun-kissed Shores

Copyright © 2025 Creative Arts Management OÜ
All rights reserved.

Author: Beckett Sinclair
ISBN HARDBACK: 978-1-80581-542-6
ISBN PAPERBACK: 978-1-80581-069-8
ISBN EBOOK: 978-1-80581-542-6

Embracing the Horizon

We danced with waves that playfully tease,
As seagulls squawk from palm tree leaves.
Flip-flops flew, oh what a sight!
Chasing crabs in the fading light.

With ice cream cones that melt too fast,
A sticky mess that's sure to last.
We laughed as sand stuck to our feet,
In this joyful, sandy retreat.

Laughter on the Coastline

A beach ball bounced, then took a dive,
Into a sunbather's peaceful hive.
He jumped up quick, his face a glare,
As kids all giggled, without a care.

Beach towels tangled, sun hats awry,
As someone's sandwich took to the sky.
We built a castle, oh so tall,
Till it crumbled down — we had a ball!

The Beach's Gentle Embrace

Our frisbee soared, then hit a guy,
Who scolded us — we all just shy.
He chased us down with furious glee,
While we just ran, too wild and free.

The waves came in with a bubbly shout,
A clam pursued us — what's that about?
With laughter loud and squeals of joy,
The ocean's charm — a playful ploy!

Warmth Beneath Our Toes

In search of shells, we scoured the sand,
While crabs plotted — oh, how they planned!
A water balloon fight erupted quick,
As laughter echoed, it's the best trick.

With sun hats flapping, we raced the tide,
Chasing waves that danced, wild and wide.
We tripped and fell, our faces bright,
In this frolicsome, joyful light.

Gleaming Waves and Golden Sands

The waves are winking, oh what a sight,
Crabs do the cha-cha, what a delight!
Seagulls gossip, with a squawk and a dive,
While sunscreen fights sand, just to survive.

Beach balls are bouncing, quite out of control,
One hit my cousin, now he's on a roll!
Flip-flops are flying, like birds on a spree,
My drink just spilled – is that just me?

Kids build castles, but they're more like mush,
As the tide creeps in, it's a frantic rush!
Shells hide in corners, making me laugh,
A crab stole my sandwich, oh what a gaffe!

As day turns to dusk, with laughter still high,
We roast marshmallows while fireflies fly.
The night will bring stories of silliness bold,
On gleaming shores, where fun never gets old!

A Journey Beneath Radiant Skies

We set off at dawn, with snacks all in tow,
The map's upside down, oh where shall we go?
Flip-flops are squeaking, my friend takes a tumble,
We laugh as we wander, our hearts in a jumble.

Ice cream is melting, drips down my chin,
I look like a clown, but I still want to win!
The sand's kind of hot, but we dance on the heat,
Every step is a giggle, it can't be beat!

Seagulls are plotting, a heist in the air,
They eye my lunch, with a keen little stare.
A wave comes a-calling, it splashes my face,
I'm soaked to the bone, but I love this mad race!

As day fades to twilight, with joy we will play,
Chasing our shadows, till the light goes away.
Underneath radiant skies, we find our bright cheer,
This journey's a memory, we'll hold it so dear!

Caress of the Daylight Tide

The waves roll in with a cheeky grin,
As seagulls dive, looking for a win.
Sandcastles crumble, the tide's big tease,
While crabs perform their funny little freeze.

With laughter echoing along the shore,
Our beach ball bounces; we all want more.
A sunburned nose, my new fashion flair,
While flip-flops dance without a care in the air.

Shimmers of Joy on Water's Edge

The surfboards wobble like we're on a spree,
Each wipeout's captured in memory.
Buckets filled with laughter, oh what a sight,
As jellyfish dance, avoiding our fright.

Now nature calls, but we're out to play,
As sunscreen battles with sweat, hooray!
We jump through waves, our feet a mere blur,
While sand sticks to us like a playful spur.

Embracing Serenity in a Coastal Dream

Shells are our treasures, but oh, the smell!
The beach was a castle; it turned to a shell.
With frolicking dolphins, a show in the sea,
They laugh at our splashes, we're all so free.

Frisbees collide, like hearts in a fling,
As laughter erupts—it's a comical thing.
We dance on the shore, our hair full of salt,
While a wave pops a beach ball, oh what a fault!

Glorious Hues at Twilight's Rise

The sunset blushes, then winks at the night,
We struggle with s'mores, a sticky delight.
Marshmallows catch fire, oh what a thrill,
As laughter and smoke begin to distill.

Chasing our shadows in the fading light,
We stumble and giggle, what a silly sight.
As stars begin twinkling, we feast with cheer,
Tomorrow's adventures, we'll hold very dear.

Blushing Skies Over Gentle Waters

The sky wore pink like a cheeky teen,
With clouds shaped like popcorn, it seemed quite keen.
The waves giggled softly, tickling the sand,
While seagulls debated, their plans were quite grand.

A sunhat was stolen by a mischievous breeze,
It danced through the air with incredible ease.
Surfboards lined up like ducks in a row,
Ready for antics where no one could go.

Nestled by the Tide

A crab in its shell wore a hat made of stripes,
It strutted along with some flamboyant vibes.
The sandcastles melted like ice in the sun,
While kids laughed and shouted, oh what fun!

Flip-flops in hand, they raced to the sea,
Tripped on their toes, oh the hilarity!
Pails turned to rockets, shovels became swords,
Imagination soared while they laughed in the fjords.

The Melody of Footprints in Soft Sand

Footprints were dancing, quite out of sync,
As waves played a tune, with a splash and a wink.
The sand tried to tickle, saying, 'Stay for a while!'
But each step they took was a laugh and a smile.

A jellyfish joked with a squishy good cheer,
Said, 'Join in the fun, it's safe over here!'
While sandpipers chirped a silly old song,
All together they danced, where the day felt so long.

Embracing the Horizon's Glow

The horizon blushed like a rosy-cheeked kid,
As waves clapped their hands, and the dolphins hid.
A picnic blanket fluttered, a kite took to flight,
With snacks on the loose, what a humorous sight!

Tongs were on duty, flipping burgers with style,
While ants held an audition, all dressed up in guile.
Laughter erupted from every direction,
The day turned to night, with giggles in collection.

Beachside Bliss Beneath Blue Skies

Sandcastles crumble, oh what a sight,
Seagulls take aim, it's a hilarious flight.
Flip-flops are flying, no one knows why,
I tripped on a crab, oh my, oh my!

Beach balls are bouncing, the kids scream with glee,
A dolphin just photobombed our selfie spree.
Ice cream's melting, drips on my nose,
Life's more fun with a popsicle pose!

Sunscreen's applied with a flick and a swirl,
But somehow I've decorated my friend, the girl.
With laughter and splashes, we dance through the foam,
Every wave whispers, "You're never alone!"

Laughter Echoes Through the Mists

Waves crash and giggles fill the warm air,
Finding a crab? Don't even dare!
As I chase a puff-ball that's racing away,
It rolled in the sand, the star of the day.

Frolicking friends all covered in sea,
Taking a photo, but wait… who's that bee?
It's buzzing around all the fun we create,
And stealing our snacks like it's the best date!

Chasing a shadow beneath the tall sun,
Someone just jumped in—now who's having fun?
With splashes and laughter, this beach is a riot,
The echoes of joy only grow in the quiet.

Secrets of the Dunes Revealed

In the dunes, we found a treasure map,
Turned out to lead to a big sunburnt chap.
He lounged on a towel, snoring so loud,
We left him a note, saying, "You're so proud!"

A sneaky sand crab scuttled by fast,
It grabbed my flip-flop, oh, what a blast!
Running for cover, I leaped like a bird,
Gathering giggles, it's what I preferred.

We dug for clams, but they all played dead,
Fighting for seaweed, who's winning instead?
Secrets unravel in each tide's embrace,
Leaving us smiling with sandy grace.

The Horizon's Embrace

Chasing the sunset, what might we find?
A flock of pink flamingos, all in a line!
They danced to the music of waves crashing near,
While I pointed and laughed, full of beachy cheer.

A kite took a flight, but not quite so grand,
It looped and it spun, losing all command.
We watched it entangle a big jellyfish,
And what a fine sight, not a single wish!

With toes in the water, we're soaking the fun,
The horizon's glowing, it's the end of the run.
But stories we'll tell will keep our hearts light,
As we braved the beach till the stars shine bright.

Radiant Reflections

The sunbeams dance on ocean's skin,
Crabs in the sand are ready to grin.
Seagulls squawk with a cheeky flair,
While kids chase waves without a care.

A dog darts past, with a ball in mouth,
Leading his friends, it's a joyful rout.
Flip-flops flying, laughter rings clear,
As ice cream drips, we all cheer!

Sunscreen slathered, a sticky delight,
Sunburned noses shining so bright.
Beach umbrellas, like mushrooms they grow,
While seagulls plot their next daring show.

Picnic sandwiches, a messy affair,
One bite too many, and crumbs everywhere!
But in this chaos, joy we will find,
With friends all around, and laughter entwined.

Horizon's Embrace

Tanning toasting like marshmallows hot,
Finding a place that's perfect, or not.
My towel's a ship anchored near the tide,
And under it, jelly sandwiches hide.

A wave just crashed, oh bless my poor hat,
It floats away like a silly old cat.
With a splash and a laugh, I dive right in,
Trying to negotiate with a crab for a win.

Dance moves in sand, oh what a faux pas,
Stumbling and laughing, we're the beach stars!
Collecting shells that look like old socks,
Naming them weird names like 'Gnasher' and 'Ox'.

As the sun slides down, colors out of line,
We toast coconut drinks with a lime twist divine.
Giggles echo as night curtains fall,
Friendships are anchored, we're having a ball!

Cerulean Dreams and Golden Gleams

A beach ball bounces, sails through the air,
But dodging it takes a bit of a dare.
Flip-flops flying in a chaotic dance,
While jellyfish waltz in their gooey romance.

Surfers are superheroes on their boards,
While sunburned tourists apply sunscreen hoards.
Sandcastles tumble, it's a sandy affair,
As a wave giggles, causing despair.

Ice cream cones wobble, the flavors are wild,
Cotton candy dreams for every young child.
Tide pools are treasures, but watch for the snails,
As laughter erupts through slip-ups and fails.

Evenings unveil the sky's twinkling sights,
We roast marshmallows and share silly flights.
Waves whisper secrets that we can't ignore,
We'll dance till the stars join the fun on the shore!

Dancing Shadows on the Beach

Shadows stretch long as the sun starts to dip,
While sand crabs take a victory trip.
Laughter erupts like a bubbly champagne,
As a toddler rolls in the soft, warm grain.

Here comes a kite, with colors that clash,
Tangled in pigtails, a bright, funny crash!
Somebody's hat is now a fish's home,
As waves chortle softly, we frolic and roam.

Sandcastles adorned with treasures like shells,
And a lost flip-flop that magically swells.
Mean while, ice cream joins the beach fun,
Melting away under rays, everyone's spun.

With a sunset finale, it's party time,
A bonfire blazing; it's almost sublime.
As the moon takes stage, we sing silly songs,
On this quirky beach, everyone belongs!

Drifting Through Morning Glories

Woke up with seagulls in my hair,
Thought they were friends, but they didn't care.
Coffee spilled on my sandy toes,
Guess that's how the morning goes.

Shells are scattered like my good sense,
Crabs are plotting in their defense.
Frolicking fish just laugh and tease,
While I sunburn my nose in ease.

Hearts Alight with Coastal Breath

Caught in a wave, a slip on my flip,
Just me and the ocean, planning a trip.
Sandcastles build with a lopsided style,
Quickly demolished by a dog with a smile.

Ice cream drips as I sprint with glee,
Sticky fingers, oh, that's just me!
A seahorse giggles, it knows my plight,
As I chase a crab under the moonlight.

The Language of Warmth and Tides

The ocean whispers, 'Why so glum?'
I respond, 'I'm here just for fun!'
Shells talk back in a salty jest,
As jellyfish float, they'll never rest.

Each wave that crashes sings a song,
Why do they declare I don't belong?
Flipping my towel, I claim my patch,
While fish are having quite the match!

Day's Embrace at the Water's Edge

Picnicking with ants — they're kind of rude,
They critiqued my sandwich and my mood.
In the distance, a kid takes a dive,
And markers on my skin shout 'live!'

Barefoot adventures are where I thrive,
Yet stepping on a crab made me revive.
As stars appear, I sing off-key,
With laughter shared and all carefree.

Moonlit Pathways of Joy

Under the moon, we dance quite silly,
We trip and tumble, oh so will ya?
The sand sticks tight to our toes with glee,
Laughing like kids, just you and me.

A crab joins in, a pinch of fun,
He waves his claws, says, "Join the run!"
We dash and dodge, like goofballs in flight,
Under the stars, it's pure delight.

With iced drinks spilled and faces aglow,
We make a mess and call it a show.
The jellyfish jig, our audience bright,
Curtains of laughter, what a night!

So here we are, in moon's bright gaze,
With every slip, we earn our praise.
Who knew the shore could bring such cheer,
A funny night, we'll always hold dear.

Tidal Whispers in the Breeze

The waves conspire, they wiggle and dance,
They splash on me, oh what a chance!
With every swish, comes a quirky splash,
Drenched from head to toe in a flash.

A seagull squawks, thinks it's a show,
Dives for fries that we tossed below.
The tide retreats, but we're not done,
We skip and sprint, pure beachside fun.

Wandering goats wear sunglasses bold,
They graze on chips, no shame to behold.
As we giggle and point, they take a stand,
Who knew goats had such a beachy band?

The breeze it whispers tales of glee,
Just in time, here come jelly, whee!
With every wave, a tale begins,
Laughing loud, let the beach games spin.

A Canvas of Light and Water

The shoreline glimmers, painted bright,
With splatter of colors, oh what a sight!
We dip our brushes, create a mess,
A canvas of joy, no need to impress.

With flops and blots, we giggle along,
The seagulls laugh, they join our song.
A splash of blue, a dab of green,
The silliest art we've ever seen.

The tide comes in, our work's erased,
We chase it back, with all due haste.
A race against art, what a delight!
The waves are laughing, we take flight.

The canvas fades but joy remains,
In every splash, we've made our gains.
Together we paint with smiles so bright,
A masterpiece born from pure delight.

Seabreeze Symphony

The breeze it whistles a cheeky tune,
As we dance like fools under the moon.
With sand in our shoes and laughter so loud,
We make a scene, oh, aren't we proud?

A crab in a bowtie takes the stage,
He struts his stuff, no hint of age.
With a pinch and a clap, he steals the show,
In this seaside concert, we steal the glow.

The waves keep time with a gentle crash,
And we waddle along, quite the splash!
A jellyfish floats, it steals the beat,
In this wacky symphony, life is sweet.

As the stars twinkle, our giggles soar,
The seabreeze carries our laughter ashore.
With waves and notes in rhythm's embrace,
This beachy serenade, our happiest place.

Dreams Woven in Salt and Sand

On the beach where seagulls squawk,
I built a castle, it looked like a rock.
It melted fast in the midday heat,
So now I hide my sand-castle defeat.

With my flip-flops on I stroll the line,
Tripping over crabs, oh what a sign!
They waddle sideways, oh what a scene,
As I laugh out loud, feeling like a queen.

The tide invites a splashing game,
As I dodge the waves, it's all so tame.
But then I slip and land with a splash,
Echoing laughter, oh what a crash!

The evening comes, with my sunburned nose,
I count the freckles—look at them grow!
With all this fun and salty cheer,
I'm the life of the beach, that's crystal clear.

Golden Hues of Dawn

The dawn peeks in with a golden flair,
I find my breakfast, a crab with a stare.
He's not impressed, just shakes his claw,
And I laugh so hard, hear the ocean's roar.

With my beach towel flapping in the breeze,
I try to nap, but the sand's full of tease.
A flock of gulls conducts a loud choir,
And I roll my eyes—wish I could retire.

The sandcastle plans go awry with glee,
As a wave sneezes, 'Achoo!'—not on me!
It topples down like my hopes and dreams,
Too much fun, or so it seems.

As golden rays dance on foamy waves,
Each moment is silly, it's what everyone craves,
With laughter and joy, that's my morning score,
Who needs any sleep? I'll just make more!

Whispering Waves at Dusk

The sun dips low, waves whisper near,
I chase a jellyfish, it's filled with cheer!
We dance on the shore, what a funny sight,
He's squishy and slimy, but I hold on tight.

With sand in my shoes, I'm feeling quite grand,
My friends gather 'round, it's a comical band.
A seagull swoops in—my sandwich it stole,
But I'm laughing too hard to care or console!

The tide rolls in, it tries to retrace,
But I land in a puddle, how's that for grace?
With every splash, the giggles explode,
A comedy sketch on this sandy road.

As dusk takes over, the stars come out,
With our sandy hair, there's no room for doubt.
We'll tell tales of bloopers, till night is done,
In this beachy laughter, we all are one.

Embrace of the Warm Breeze

The warm breeze hugs me like old friends,
While sand sticks to me, oh how it bends.
I wear a hat—but it flies away,
Chasing it like it's some silly play!

My sunblock's thick, I look like a ghost,
But it's supposed to help, that's what I boast.
A child nearby, with a bucket in hand,
Dumps water on my feet, oh what a stand!

With laughter escaping as waves jump high,
A frisbee sails past, oh me, oh my!
I duck and I dodge, just to fit the game,
But land on my back, the sand's got no shame.

The day winds down, we share goofy tales,
As the wind whispers softly, it never fails.
With love and laughter, we gather and cheer,
On this beachy playground, joy is so clear!

Waves of Serenity

The beach ball flew with a great big plop,
Landing right where the seagulls hop.
Kids laugh and run, dodging wet sand,
While parents nap with a drink in hand.

A crab in a hat danced near the shore,
Claiming the sandcastle, wanting more.
The tide tickles toes, shows no respect,
With waves making shorts an odd suspect.

Saltwater Serenades

A fish with a whistle sings on a rock,
While a clam does a jig, oh what a shock!
Flip-flops are flinging, lost in the breeze,
As laughter joins in like a jolly tease.

Seashells are treasures, or so they say,
But most just find them to toss and play.
With sand stuck in hair, a funny whole crew,
Ocean's antics, quite a view!

The Glow of Twilight Tides

As twilight glimmers, waves clink like mugs,
Fish wearing shades are giving out hugs.
A dolphin pops up with a splashy grin,
Sporting a surfboard, the fun's about to begin!

The moon's got a glow, like a giant lamp,
While beach-goers roast marshmallows, happy camp.
A seagull steals fries, that crafty old lad,
As a toddler just giggles, isn't that mad!

Caressed by the Ocean's Breath

The breeze whispers jokes, tickling our ears,
As grandpa starts dancing, shedding some tears.
With a towel for a cape, he struts with pride,
While grandma throws shade, with gossip as guide.

A juggler of shells draws quite the crowd,
With seagulls as critics, cheering out loud.
Laughter drifts high, like kites in the blue,
At this funny beach, there's viel to pursue!

Reflections of Joy on the Coast

On sandy strips, we dance and play,
With seagulls stealing fries away.
Flip-flops fly, it's quite a show,
Who needs a beach ball, just let's go!

The sun is bright, but so are we,
Chasing crabs, we squeal with glee.
Buckets spill, our castle's a mess,
Turns out sand weighs more, who would guess?

Ice cream drips down, oh no, it's gone,
Laughter echoes, from dusk till dawn.
We splash and fall, it's quite a sight,
Life's simple joys feel just so right.

Horizons Wrapped in Warmth

Waves whisper tales of salty fun,
Sunburned noses and giggles run.
Frisbees flying, oh what a throw,
Last seen by a kid who said, 'Whoa!'

Seashells gathered, treasures to find,
Each one's a mystery, one of a kind.
We seek them out with frantic zest,
Why does the crab look so unimpressed?

Picnic spreads on a blanket wide,
Sandwiches squished, joy can't be denied.
With every bite, there's laughter anew,
How do we manage to spill so true?

The Magic of Incoming Waves

Waves crash down with a splosh and a pop,
We run away, then roll right back up!
Sandcastle fortresses rise with pride,
Till a wave crashes in, a watery slide.

The tide pulls back, oh what a tease,
Making footprints, sweeping with ease.
Then it holes right in, the footprints are lost,
Did I just step where the sea's gonna toss?

Belly flops grace the shoreline's edge,
Impact's huge! We leap from a ledge.
Each splash we make is quite the cheer,
Though I think that was a fish, oh dear!

Where Sea Meets Sunkissed Thoughts

Summer vibes wrapped in salty air,
Collecting moments without a care.
Towels spread out, snacks we explore,
Did someone say potato chips galore?

With laughter echoing on the breeze,
Chasing shadows, it's sure to please.
Sun hats perched, look at us go,
One flip and—oops!—down I throw!

Bubbles floating high in the sky,
We wave and giggle, oh me, oh my!
With every giggle, the world feels bright,
Who knew joy could make such a sight?

Timeless Dance of Sand and Surf

The waves are a playful bunch,
As they tickle toes and lunch.
Seagulls squawk with no finesse,
Performing their own comic mess.

Buckets and shovels in a race,
Sandcastles fall without a trace.
A crab sidesteps without care,
As if he's dancing, unaware!

Laughter echoes with each splash,
And sandy clothes make quite the clash.
Flip-flops fly, a wild affair,
While sunscreen's lotion ends up where?

But in this glorious, sunny nook,
Life's a fun, unending book.
With giggles in the salty air,
And memories that float everywhere!

Daydreams Drifting in the Breeze

A beach chair creaks, a snack in hand,
The seagulls plot, oh isn't it grand?
Falling asleep, I miss my tan,
Woken by a wayward sandman.

In my dreams, I'm a mermaid queen,
With starfish crowns and glimmering sheen.
But reality bites like gritty grit,
As I sip my drink, and a straw won't fit.

The water's warm, the fun's on tap,
Kids run past; watch out for the flap!
Splash zones claimed by squeals and yells,
With laughter in waves, who needs shells?

As daylight fades, the BBQ starts,
Charred hot dogs add comedic parts.
Evenings dance, with fireflies' flares,
Creating fun in the salty airs!

Shores of Softly Blushing Twilight

As the sun dips low, we gather near,
With snacks and smiles, and summer cheer.
An awkward stumble, quite the show,
As I trip and drop my ice cream, oh no!

Twilight paints the horizon gold,
While the stories of the day unfold.
A dog steals burgers with his charm,
Leaving us with gut-busting alarm!

Kites soar high, too close—oh dear!
Caught in my hair, it's now a spear.
Sun hats drift off like lazy boats,
While laughter rings from all sorts of quotes.

As stars peek out, we roast some treats,
With chocolate gooey and sticky sweets.
In this rosy glow of evening's song,
We laugh together, where we belong!

Whispers of the Ocean's Heart

The ocean waves whisper to my feet,
With each tickle, it's a sandy greet.
Oops, there goes my drink, off the edge,
Now a jellyfish guards my pledge!

Fishermen cast with the strongest lore,
But all they catch are seaweed galore.
Kids chase crabs on a big, bold quest,
While I just try to spot a seagull's nest.

The tide rolls out, sadness ensues,
With footprints washing away my blues.
But here comes a splash, unexpected delight,
As the water fights back with all its might!

With buckets and shovels, all is well,
As the day wraps up in this sandy shell.
In playful waves and laughter's spree,
We find joy in every silly decree!

Tides of Luminous Delight

Beaches so bright, oh what a sight,
Seagulls gossip, flying with delight.
Buckets and shovels all around,
Building castles, but they fall down!

Waves wave back with a foamy cheer,
Splashing our fun, we laugh without fear.
Sandy snacks go missing in a blur,
Maybe a crab thought it was dessert!

Sunscreen smeared like a clumsy art,
Sticky fingers, where do I start?
Flip-flops dance to a silly beat,
Every grain's a bit of trapped heat!

As we chase the tide, taking a spin,
Footprints mingle, where do we begin?
Laughter echoes under sky so bright,
Tides retreat but the fun feels right!

Radiant Reflections in the Sand

Sunshine glistens on a shimmering sea,
Waving to jellyfish, so carefree.
Sandy hair and sunscreen eyes,
We giggle at buckets as the tide does rise.

Squirt guns ready, watch out, beware!
Splashing around like we haven't a care.
A beach ball bounces, a dog gives chase,
Who knew the ocean could hold such a race?

Shiny shells hide jokes in their curves,
Telling tales that leave us with swerves.
Flip-flops fly when we run out of blame,
Only to find that we're all the same!

Picnic time with sandwiches spread,
A seagull swoops, our lunch feels dread.
But laughter carries on like a tune,
Another bite lost to the beach buffoon!

The Dance of Light and Sea

Salt in the air, a waltz of delight,
Sun hats wobble under the bright light.
Beach towels flutter, a colorful show,
Much like my attempt at a limbo low!

Waves whisper secrets as we twirl and swerve,
Flip-flops fly as we try to conserve.
Ice cream cones, oh dear, what a mess,
When it drips down, it's anyone's guess!

As tides come in with a bubbly cheer,
We chase after fun with giggles sincere.
A crab snaps back, it thought I was food,
Now we dance with more laughter, so good!

Seashells clanking like a funny band,
Naps forgotten in the golden sand.
Every heartbeat syncs with the flow,
In this dance of waves, we steal the show!

Warmth Cradled by Ocean's Touch

Sandcastles plush, like pillows they stand,
Each wave that crashes, a mischievous hand.
Splashing our friends with a playful tease,
Running like kids, hearts light as a breeze.

Sunshine's a friend, though it makes us glow,
Check out my tan line, but don't look too slow!
Belly flop contests bring cheers and jeers,
Gleeful laughter drowns out our fears.

Surfboards tumble, oops, into the sea,
The ocean just giggles, come play with me!
Fried calamari makes us giggle and sigh,
Why does it wink at our ketchup fry?

Shells squabble gossip, a crustacean tale,
Seagulls compete for the ultimate fail.
Warmth envelops us, a blanket of fun,
In this seaside jest, we are never done!

A Treasure of Sunlit Whispers

Seagulls squawk like they own the place,
Chasing tourists with a cheeky grace.
Beach towels tangled, like spaghetti knots,
Now everyone's laughing at their sunburned spots.

Ice cream drips down a toddler's chin,
A sticky mess with a goofy grin.
Parents fumble with sand in their shoes,
While their kids dig holes like mini-august blues.

Buckets and spades in a chaotic pile,
Creatures resembling castles, with a wink and a smile.
The tide comes in, and all hope is lost,
But it's just another adventure; let's not count the cost.

So grab your shades and a frosty drink,
Wish the seagulls would learn to think.
In this sandy circus, laughter's the score,
Every misstep turns into folklore!

Glimmers of Dreamscapes at Dusk

Footprints fade as the waves sing low,
Dancing shadows put on quite a show.
Bikini tops, a fashion disaster,
Even the crabs are laughing faster.

A sandcastle army, all ready to fight,
But the tide has plans; it's set for tonight.
Sunscreen battles that leave quite a mess,
Look, there's Uncle Bob, in his full-body dress!

The evening breeze tickles the nose,
As everyone tries to pose with their toes.
Fireworks above, fizzing like soup,
Hoping no one jumps up and trips the loop.

So, let's toast to the moments so weird,
Where even the dolphins might meet a beard.
With laughter and joy, we can surely trust,
Life on the coast is a bit off the bust!

Twilight's Embrace on Weathered Rocks

The rocks are slippery; we're all on a quest,
But the wind's made it clear, it's a crazy fest.
Old Timmy slips, oh what a sight,
Like a fish on land, giving us fright!

The crabs throw a party, they're in on the fun,
With pinching contests—they'll not be outdone.
"Watch your toes!" warns a girl with a laugh,
As a rogue wave arrives, stealing her staff.

Sunsets glow in hues of odd,
Matching the pink of Aunt May's old bod.
Champagne corks popping, with flair in the dusk,
"It's a beach bash!" we all cheer, with a husk.

By the fire, we share tales, both big and small,
Of jellyfish dances and seagull brawls.
With laughter and warmth, we'll claim our place,
Forever the misfits of this rocky space!

The Eternal Greeting of Wave and Shore

Waves go whoosh, like an over-excited friend,
They crash, retreat, and then they pretend.
Sandcastles crumble, a royal decree,
As kids shout, "Hey! That was royalty!"

The weathered beach chair's lost in the mix,
With grandpa snoozing—what a funny fix!
A Frisbee flies past, like a rogue bird,
And lands right in someone's juicy curd.

Barbecues sizzle with too much corn,
While seagulls plot how to steal the adorn.
A picnic table tipped over in style,
All join in laughter, a comical trial.

So we raise our glasses to this beachy sight,
Where fun and mishaps are always in flight.
With waves that greet us, a wild rapport,
Here's to the chaos, let's ask for more!

Golden Sands at Dusk

At the beach, I lost my shoe,
Now I've got just one to view.
The crabs are laughing as they scurry,
I chase them down, but they're in a hurry.

With ice cream drips on my new hat,
I sit down, and we both chat.
A seagull swoops, snatches my fries,
He flies off, and I shout surprise!

The waves keep pulling, always in tug,
Sandcastles crumbling, giving a shrug.
I add a shell, declare it a throne,
But now my artwork's all alone.

As twilight comes, I start to dance,
Tripping over my own pants.
Laughter echoes 'til the night,
Oh, beach days are pure delight!

Whispering Waves and Warm Breezes

I went for a walk, my hat flew far,
Chased it down, hit a beach bar.
Ordered a drink, then saw it float,
In my cup? My hat took a soak!

The breeze is playful, flipping my dress,
Sand in my sandwich, I must confess.
Seagulls squawking their best comic bits,
While I'm just hoping for some cool hits.

The tide rolls in with a comical splash,
Upside down, my flip-flops crash.
I laugh as they vanish, what a fine joke,
As the ocean's giggles fill the yoke.

With friends by my side, we play and tease,
Building weird towers with utmost ease.
Beach days fly, but we stay in glee,
For nothing's as silly as waiting on the sea.

Tides of Radiance

The tide rolled in with a funny sound,
Caught my towel, it spun around.
I chased it down like a mad sprint,
Thought I saw a dolphin, but it was a flint.

Sunburned noses and ice cream smiles,
We draw funny faces in the sand tiles.
A crab joins in, he's quite the painter,
Splashing colors while dodging a gainer.

I built a beach ball, it was quite grand,
Until it popped, and I lost it in hand.
The chase was on, laughter all night,
In this silly place, everything's bright.

As stars twinkle, we tell our tales,
Of flying hats and tidal wails.
Together we laugh, it's a comic spree,
These golden hours, truly carefree!

Where the Light Meets the Sea

Waves whisper secrets, funny and clear,
I caught a fish, and it laughed at me, dear.
Tried to take a selfie, with glimmers aglow,
But ended up drenched, what a hapless show!

Friends dress up in shells, a fashion parade,
Sunglasses on, they start to trade.
A wiggly worm tries to steal the scene,
But in the end, I ate a jelly bean.

As dusk draws near, my drink goes dry,
So I fill it again, hoping to fly.
Λ crumply chipmunk joins our feast,
With little hands, it manages a least!

We roast marshmallows, but they melt fast,
S'mores turn into a sticky, fun blast!
With laughter and warmth, we all agree,
This is the spot where joy runs free!

Celestial Hues in Soft Ocean Air

The sky wears a smile, oh what a sight,
With beach balls bouncing, it feels just right.
Seagulls are squawking, looking so proud,
While sunbathers dance in the sun's warm crowd.

Flip-flops play tag, it's all quite absurd,
Sandy toes wiggle, like they're disturbed.
A crab in a top hat struts with such flair,
This beach day is wild—beyond compare!

Kites are like rainbows, high up they soar,
While kids chase the waves, who could ask for more?
A picnic's in motion, but oh what a fail,
When seagulls unite to snatch up the trail!

As daylight fades, laughter fills the bay,
Frolicking under the colors of play.
With joy in the air, we toast our good cheer,
These silly beach moments bring us all near.

Waves of Warm Sunshine

In sunlight we frolic, what a silly spree,
Splashing in waves, feeling so free.
The dog steals our sandwiches—oh what a prank,
While surfers are toppled, oh how we tank!

The water's a giggle, it tickles your toes,
With surfboards like fish, they wiggle and pose.
A splash fight erupts, it's chaos and glee,
With laughter that echoes like a wild spree.

Umbrellas go flying, tumbling round,
Beach chairs in chaos, some haven't been found.
We're dodging the volleyball, counting to ten,
Just to get smacked by a rogue wave again!

As sun sinks to rest, the twilight's our stage,
With sunscreen and giggles, we act like a sage.
The sand sticks to laughter, it's all quite benign,
These moments of joy are our favorite sign.

Memories Written in the Sand

With shovels like scepters, they dig and they build,
Castles of dreams, oh how they are filled!
A moat turns to mud, as tides start to creep,
And children all giggle, they're not ready to sleep.

Each footprint a secret, trails left behind,
With the tide as the thief, how cruel but so kind!
They draw funny faces, they'll wash out of sight,
With the moon soon arriving to sprinkle the night.

A shell turned to jewel, collects all the praise,
While crabs steal the stage with their clumsy ballet.
A picnic invasion, oh where did it go?
Seagulls hold court like they're all in the show!

The sunset's a canvas, we wave goodbye blissed,
With laughter and whispers, impossibly missed.
Memories fade softly like each tiny grain,
But we'll never forget this wild, sandy reign.

Shores that Hold Secrets

At the edge of the world, where laughter does tumble,
Secrets are hiding, yet they only mumble.
A flip-flop stands guard, taking its vow,
While dolphins conspire to steal every wow.

Old beach towels wrinkled from sunbathing fame,
Chat with the crabs, they all know your name.
A jellyfish chuckles, it's hard not to jest,
While starfish high-five as they dance with the best.

Footprints pretend drama, deep in the sand,
Each tells a story of a small, silly band.
As the tide tells its tale on this vast, sandy floor,
We gather the giggles and rush back for more.

Even the waves, with their fabled spree,
Secrets are whispered, they'll never be free.
With shells as our witnesses and laughter our song,
We revel in humor where we all belong.

Quilts of Clouds and Seafoam

Puffy clouds drift like pillows,
While seagulls snatch fries from fellows,
Waves crash and giggle like old friends,
At twilight, the laughter never ends.

Beach balls bounce in a silly dance,
Flip-flops flying, an awkward prance,
Children chase crabs, oh what a sight,
Tails wiggling left, while they run right!

Sunscreen applied, yet laughter's the glue,
A sunscreen war, splatters of white goo,
Our sandy masterpieces grow in the night,
Beach beauticians—funny, but just right!

The horizon blends with a pineapple drink,
"Salty hair, don't care!" as we all wink,
These shorelines are mischief, a patchwork delight,
With quilts of mischief, all feels just right.

The Art of Ocean's Caress

The ocean's embrace is a warm, wet hug,
Belly flops diving like a rubber rug,
Waves toss us about, laughter in tow,
The sand's a better seat than old Joe's slow glow.

We grab our boards, oh what a sight!
Surfing the foam, with all of our might,
But every tumble brings squeals of cheer,
"Hey, let's do that again!" as we all disappear!

Seashells sing songs of lost pirate gold,
But we find old flip-flops, now weathered and old,
The prize is a joke, but laughter's the key,
Who knew beachcombing could crack you with glee?

As tide pulls its tricks, we're swept all around,
With giggles and splashes, let joy abound,
The ocean is wild, yet tames every "whoops,"
While we dive into whimsy and warm sandy loops.

Sacred Spaces of Silver Sands

Golden feet dance on sparkling grains,
Sandy sandwiches add to our gains,
Our towels are forts from the sun's glaring eyes,
As we battle the breeze with comical sighs.

Kites dive and swoop like they own the sky,
While dogs notice frogs and chase them awry,
We watch the battles unfold with chortles,
As crabby competitors crowd their new portals.

Beach bingo, the sand is the board,
Finding lost things, our merriment's stored,
Like flip-flops tangled in someone's long hair,
Who knew beach games could lead to such flair?

Here lies our patch of misfit delight,
Where snacks become treasures, all feel so right,
As laughter rings out, the day drifts away,
Like playing at whimsy in a bright cabaret.

Daybreak Dreams Ebbing Away

Morning sun peeks like an eager kid,
Our sleepy heads nod, "Oh, let's not forbid!"
Coffee spills over like tides on the shore,
With giggles and yawns, we're craving much more.

Castles are built with moats of pure glee,
But watch out for waves—oh look, there goes Lee!
His great architecture meets a watery fate,
Yet each splash brings laughter—we still celebrate!

Seagulls swoop in, oh what a ruckus,
Stealing our snacks, they create a big fuss,
As we giggle and barter our treats with the tide,
"Okay, you take chips, while I'll take your fried!"

The day fades to dusk, but still we hold tight,
As the moon winks down, all feels just right,
With laughter and stories, we cherish the stay,
In dreams of the ocean, we'll drift far away.

Echoes of Seagulls' Serenade

Upon the beach, they squawk and play,
Chasing crumbs like children at bay.
With beaks so bold and eyes so bright,
They steal my fries in plain daylight.

A gull took off with my sandwich neat,
Leaving me here with a soggy seat.
I waved my hands, shouted in vain,
But he simply laughed, soaring insane.

Their laughter echoes, a raucous tune,
Underneath the lazy afternoon.
I think I'll stick to chips and dip,
For gulls are good at the swoop and zip.

So here I sit with a sunburned nose,
Amused by antics that nobody knows.
A beachside feast for feathered fiends,
Life's a comedy on golden gleams.

Drifting Amongst Amber Curls

Waves with laughter, so soft and sweet,
Scooping up seashells, a sandy treat.
I tripped on a crab who danced with flair,
He pinched my toe without any care.

Seashells lined up, all in a row,
Each a treasure, but I'm moving slow.
I found a starfish, took him for a ride,
He waved goodbye, then fell to the tide.

The wind whispers secrets, the sun's a tease,
Tickling my nose with a careless breeze.
I tried to catch sand in a soggy sack,
It slipped away, what a silly knack!

As tumbleweeds laugh on the shore,
I join their giggles, who could ask for more?
A day of jest on this amber curl,
With every wave, the humor will unfurl.

The Canvas of Coastal Lullabies

Brush strokes of blue against the sand,
Dancing crabs form a marching band.
I joined their frolic, forgot my woes,
Until my flip-flop took a nosedive, who knows?

Buckets of laughter, splashes afloat,
A fish swam by in a tiny boat.
I shouted, "Hey! Come join the fun!"
It leaped in surprise; now we're on the run!

Seagulls giggle, their beaks are bright,
In a silly game of sea-salt flight.
I tried to join, but flapped my arms wide,
Ended with splashes right by the tide.

So here I find, with a heart so light,
Coastal moments, a pure delight.
A canvas painted with giggles and song,
Where nature's humor just doesn't seem wrong.

Treasures in the Tidal Pool

Puddles of secrets, reflections of glee,
I spotted a crab doing the cha-cha with me.
He winked and he danced, oh, such a sight,
In a tidal pool party, we sparked delight.

A seaweed wig had me in stitches,
As fishy friends pulled some silly glitches.
I tried to swim, but slipped on a shell,
Flipped like a pancake, oh what a swell!

The tide comes in with a splash and a roar,
While my new pals dance on the ocean floor.
I joined their jigs, in my quirky style,
Who knew that sea stars could dance with such guile?

So gather 'round, for a show like no other,
Where bubbly laughter makes all souls smother.
In aquatic magic, let the fun unfurl,
With treasures found, let's give it a whirl!

Dance of the Sunbeams on the Sea

The waves do a jig, so spry and light,
Shells wear sun hats, what a funny sight!
Fish in tuxedos swim left and right,
As seagulls laugh, it's pure delight.

Crabs in a conga, rocking the tide,
With a splash and a twirl, they take great pride!
The dolphins join in, not one to hide,
Under bright rays, they dance side by side.

Beach balls bounce high, with a pop and a cheer,
As sunbeams wiggle, they start to steer,
Laughter erupts, from far and near,
Ocean's own party, oh my dear!

With flip-flops and giggles, the day flies by,
Under whimsical clouds, we'll wave goodbye,
A memory made, like a sweet pie,
Pak in our bags, the fun doesn't die!

Tidal Dreams in Golden Embrace

Waves whisper secrets of dreams untold,
While starfish in dresses shine bright and bold,
Seashells giggle, their stories unfold,
In patches of sand, they discover gold.

Crabs in a line, like a marching band,
Stomp to the rhythm of the swirling sand,
Fish toss confetti, oh how they planned,
Under the watch of the fun-loving land.

Kites in the wind, they dance and they twirl,
With laughter and joy, they give a whirl,
The tide takes a break, gives a gentle curl,
As beach bums lounge, with hair in a swirl.

Ice creams drip down, a curious sight,
With coconut laughs and sprinkles of light,
We chase off the crabs in a comical fright,
While dreaming of tides that sparkle all night!

Horizon's Promise at Daybreak

The sun peeks over, tickling the waves,
While turtles in sunglasses act like they braves,
A lobster parade in a line like knaves,
With giggles and snorts, that's how they behave!

Birds play charades, with squawks of delight,
They strut down the beach, with all of their might,
Shell necklaces glimmer, oh what a sight,
As day's open arms hold laughter so tight.

Sandcastles rise up, in mystical air,
With moats for the crabs, they need a good scare,
The tide's feeling cheeky, a mischievous pair,
As seaweed wigs flutter, we all stop and stare.

As bright as a penny, the day starts to shine,
With funny hats on, we toast to the line,
Here's to the misfits, where spirits entwine,
At this beach of dreams, we say we are fine!

Sunlit Memories on Sandy Solitude

Each grain of sand, stories in tow,
With seagulls who gossip, they steal the show,
Starfish are dancing, in a quiet row,
While crabs trade jokes, just thought you should know!

Buckets of laughter spill over the shore,
As beach balls collide, they start a rapport,
Tidal tickles and splashes galore,
Where laughter and joy just continue to pour.

The penguins in bow ties, really quite grand,
Join conga lines formed in the warm golden sand,
A party of sea life, so perfectly planned,
Together they prance, hand in fin, hand in hand.

With sandy toes wiggling, we bask in the glow,
As fuzzy iguanas start stealing the show,
Memories woven, like threads in a row,
In this silly paradise, we surely will grow!

Glimmers on the Horizon

A crab in a tux, oh what a sight,
He dances the cha-cha, under the light.
Seagulls gossip like they have a plan,
While waves roll in, with a laugh, they span.

In flip-flops we stumble, on sandy terrain,
Chasing each other, it's all just a game.
The beach ball bounces like it's on a spree,
And sunscreen fights back, oh, wild jubilee!

Dolphins join in with a playful flip,
They greet our antics, as we take a dip.
A seagull swoops down, to steal a fry,
And we all erupt with a bubbly sigh.

As the day fades away, we're all in a blur,
Collecting our shells, laughter's the cure.
With ice cream in hand, we walk home to rest,
What a weird day, it was simply the best!

Salted Air

Whiff of the ocean, a whacky deodorant,
That seagulls wear proudly, it's quite adamant.
Sandy toes wiggling, feeling so free,
Except when the tide comes to tickle my knee.

Mermies are real, I swear I just saw,
One trading a shell for a good old straw.
They giggle and splash, with a giddy delight,
The beach is alive, what a comical sight!

As I chase after seagulls, they give me the slip,
And I trip on my towel – what a crazy trip!
Yet sunbathers smile, while sipping their drink,
For who wouldn't laugh at a wild splash and wink?

Caught up in the chaos of all that's in sway,
I find joy in sandcastles, made of clay.
It's salty and sweet, like a nutty surprise,
At the beach, nothing's serious, just fun in disguise!

Soft Skin

Lathered in lotion, like butter on bread,
Trying to tan, but end up red instead.
The lifeguard is snickering, watching the scene,
As I wriggle like jelly, it's quite the routine!

Covered in sand, I'm a walking dessert,
My friends laugh aloud, asserting the dirt.
With beach hats like towers, we strut with flair,
Oh, the sights we create, it's a fashion affair!

A seagull approaches, perhaps here for a snack,
With popcorn in hand, I'm ready for attack.
But it snatches my treat, like it's part of the plan,
And I just stand there, with a wide-open span!

Soft skin gets sticky from salt and the sun,
Yet these silly moments are simply pure fun.
With giggles and splashes, we embrace every flaw,
It's life at the beach, where we laugh and just thaw!

A Palette of Nature's Crème

Squeezed lemon laughter, as we sip lemonade,
Mixed with the sound of a comical parade.
A rainbow of beach balls bounces and rolls,
While we chase our dreams in flip-flops and strolls.

Cotton candy clouds float above our hair,
As we mingle like jellybeans, without a care.
The color of sunsets, we wear like a crown,
And sunset selfies? Yeah, we act like a clown!

Kite strings entangle like a clumsy ballet,
While I dodge a rogue frisbee, come what may.
My shade is a towel, and I'm feeling so grand,
But not as grand as that sunburned man!

With laughter like waves on the shoreline so bright,
We savor our moments, from morning till night.
Brush strokes of fun on this canvas so wide,
In this gallery of joy, come on, take pride!

Gentle Waves

Waves tickle my toes, a slippery tease,
Splashing my laughter, like the lightest breeze.
With each goofy tumble, I'm the beach clown,
As my friends start to giggle, not letting me down!

Sandcastles crumble like wishful regret,
But my dreams are afloat, like a quirky duet.
Mermaids in shells, oh they're rolling their eyes,
At our sandy shenanigans in silly disguise.

A floating beach towel, my regal throne,
As I wave to the folks, like I'm not alone.
Yet gulls are all plotting, to snatch up my chip,
And I'm left here wondering, was that a fair flip?

But life's never serious, not here on the coast,
With snickers of joy, oh, we happily boast.
Let the waves carry us, with laughter anew,
In this bubble of mirth, we'll always renew!

Bright Memories

With sunglasses perched, I squint at the sea,
Where laughter is plenty, and chaos runs free.
Every return a wild beach ball thrown high,
Memories crafted, like kites in the sky.

In the distance, a dog – oh, what a convolute,
Chasing after waves, proudly wearing his suit.
We cheer for the moments that time can't replace,
Finding humor in beach sands, and all in our chase.

Ice cream's a drippy delight, a splash in my lap,
While once was a scoop, now it's part of my map.
The flavor of laughter, a swirl in our smile,
As we wade through the joy, it's totally worthwhile!

At the end of the day, as we dry in the sun,
We share all our stories, and know we've had fun.
For treasures are made of laughter and cheer,
In the album of life, day by day, year by year!

www.ingramcontent.com/pod-product-compliance
Lightning Source LLC
Chambersburg PA
CBHW072133070526
44585CB00016B/1650